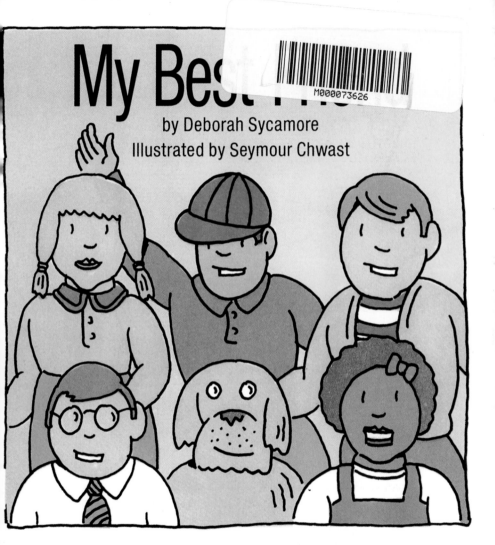

My Best

by Deborah Sycamore
Illustrated by Seymour Chwast

CELEBRATION PRESS
Pearson Learning Group

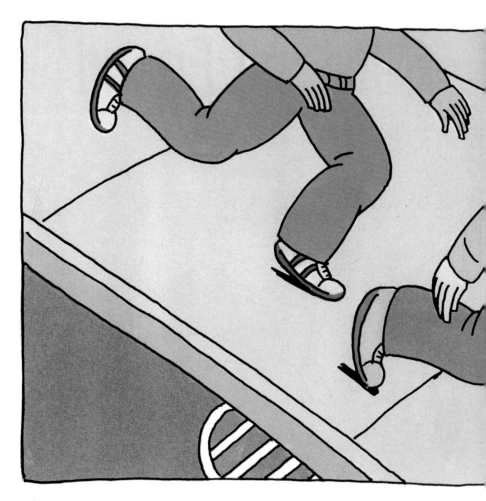

I like to run.

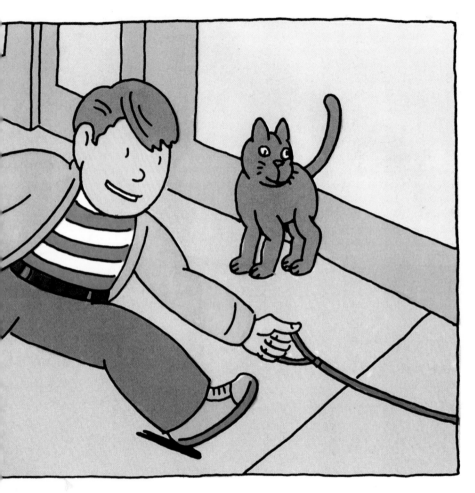

So does Joey.

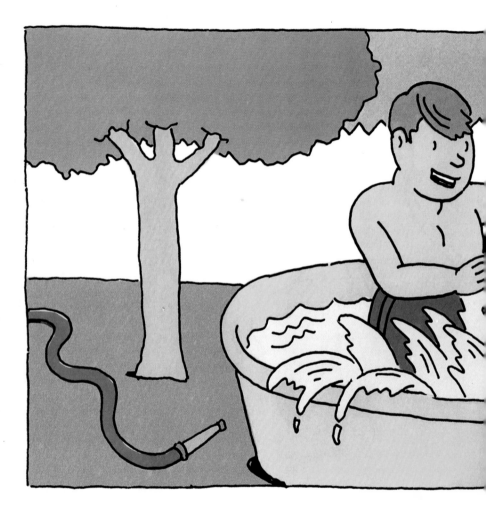

I like to swim.

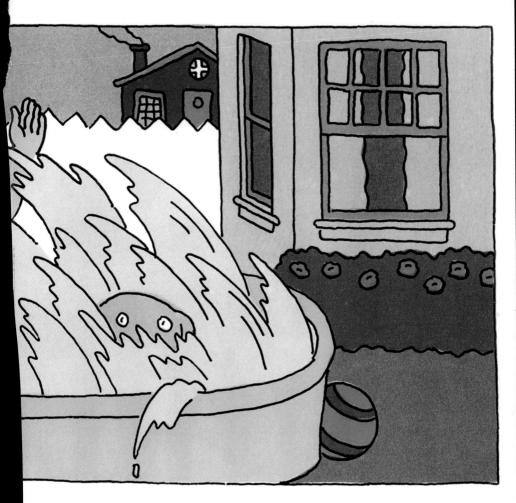

So does Joey.

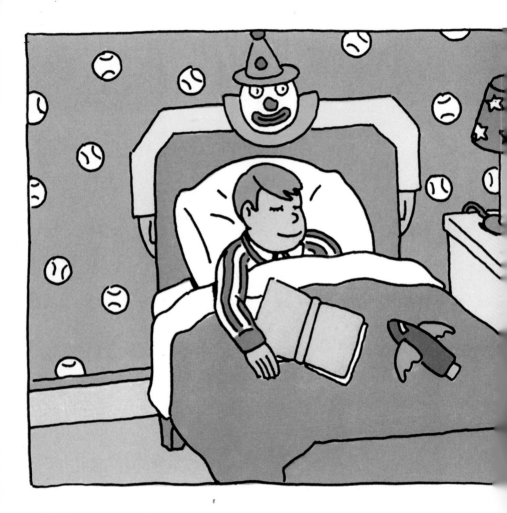

I like to sleep.

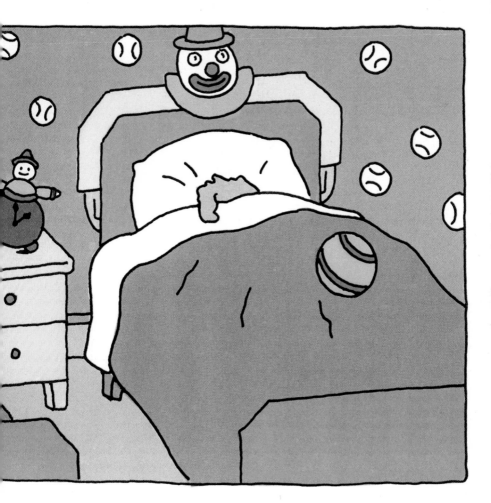

So does Joey.

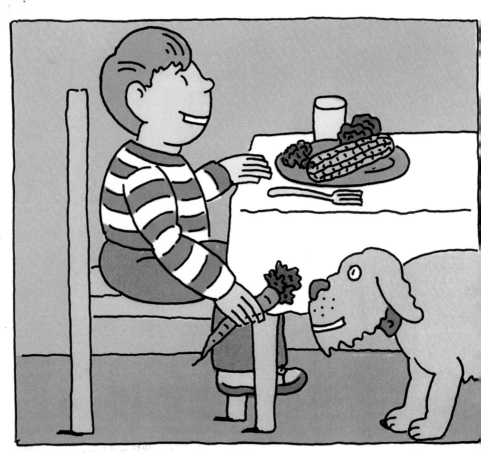

Joey likes vegetables.

He's my best friend.